TWENTY ONE

BIBLICAL PROPHETIC DECLARATIONS

TO SPEAK OVER YOUR LIFE

ELDER STEVIE BARNETT

Chain Publishing
Jamaica, W.I.
Copyright © 2023 Stevie Barnett

land, your animals, and your business and receive your blessings. God said it, we believe it and it is done. Amen

DAY FOUR

According to Deuteronomy 28:5, I decree and declare that "my basket and my store shall be blessed"

Complete affirmation four.

Psalm 23:1a says, *"The Lord is my shepherd I shall not want"*. As a result of Him being our Shepherd, we will not lack basic needs such as food, shelter, and clothing. Our basket shall be blessed with food. We will have enough to store even for a rainy day and to share with others.

There was a young man who worked faithfully in the Ministry for many years, during that time he held many positions in the church. He was always kind and willing to give out of what the Lord has blessed him with. The young brother lost his job and had a family to feed. During the time he was out of a job, he and his family did not go to bed hungry. God opened the windows of heaven and poured on him and his family blessings, pressed down, shaken together, and running over.

At one point a person went to a foreign land with the intention to return, the person packed two barrels with food and other basic supplies.

Somehow the person decided to stay in that country and decided to send those two barrels of food and other supplies to the young man and his family. They had food enough for weeks.

When I was young I heard a story of a widow who had no food. She prayed and asked God to send her food. Acting on faith, she placed the pot of water on the stove and waited. When the water came to a boil she heard a knocking. When she went to the door a friend was there with a bag of groceries. She was able to prepare a meal for herself and her family. From these examples, we see that God will make a way even when there seems to be no way. He is an on-time God. He may not come when you want Him but He will show up on time.

A few days ago I was watching Trinity Broadcasting Network (TBN) and the preacher told a story about a woman who had no food and God provided for her through an unexpected source. In summary, the story goes like this "There was an atheist who was neighbor to an old Christian lady. The Christian lady would always give thanks with a load voice for all God has done for her. She was loud enough for the atheist to hear. As time went by, the old Christian lady fell on hard times and of course she prayed aloud and asked God for food.

The atheist heard her praying with her request for food. Listening to her prayers, the atheist devised a plan to prove to the old lady that there was indeed no God. He bought two bags of groceries and, after placing them on her porch, he rang her bell and then hid in some nearby bushes. When the old woman came out of her house, she saw the bags of groceries and started giving thanks to the Lord for sending her the food. At that point, the happy atheist jumped from the bushes and shouted, "AH-HA! The Lord didn't send you those groceries! It was I who put them there!!!!"

Without a pause, the old woman shot back, "PRAISE YOU, DEAR LORD. NOT ONLY DID YOU SEND THE GROCERIES, BUT YOU ALSO MADE THE DEVIL PAY FOR THEM!"

God is a Good Shepherd (John 10:11). God is a Great Shepherd (Hebrews 13: 20, 21). God is the Chief Shepherd (1st Peter 5:4). If you call on Him and decree and declare that your basket and store is blessed, He will continue to supply your basic needs and more.

DAY FIVE

According to Deuteronomy 28:6, I decree and declare that "I shall be blessed when I goest out and when I comest in"

Complete affirmation five.

Blessing is a way of life for those who believe and live according to the principles of God. Our God is the King of Kings and the Lord of Lords. He is the conquering Lion of the Tribe of Judah. There is no limit to God's blessings to those who truly love Him, to those who truly keep His commandments. Matthew 22: 37-40 says *"Jesus said unto him, Thou shalt love the Lord thy God with all thy heart, and with all thy soul, and with all thy mind. This is the first and great commandment. And the second is like unto it, Thou shalt love thy neighbor as thyself. On these two commandments hang all the law and the prophets.*

If we show love to God and others there is no limit to the blessings we will receive from God in **all** aspects of our lives (He has provided every blessing—health, prosperity, peace of mind, joy, deliverance from sin and everything that pertains to our good life – 2nd Peter 1:3).

Job was blessed in his going out and his coming in because he was perfect and upright, and one who feared God and eschewed evil (Job 1:1) Job was blessed with a family, assets and friends and was described as the greatest of all the men of the east.

To confidently decree and declare this blessing over your life start by loving God and loving people and the sky is the limit to what you can achieve. So go now and do what you must to access all the blessings stored up for you in the Kingdom of God.

David spoke these words when God delivered him out of the hands of Saul. David had a personal relationship with God and like the Good Shepherd, the Lord was always there to protect him. Once you have a relationship with God, you don't have to fear when trouble comes your way. **2 Chronicles 20:15** says *"And he said, Hearken ye, all Judah, and ye inhabitants of Jerusalem, and thou king Jehoshaphat, Thus saith the Lord unto you, Be not afraid nor dismayed by reason of this great multitude; for the battle is not yours, but God's"*. Leave the fighting to God. In this text, we see where several enemies came against Jehoshaphat but Jehoshaphat seek the face of the Lord and proclaimed a fast.

The Lord then instructed them to worship. The worshipers went ahead of the army and the praise and worship confused the enemies and they killed each other.

Similarly, to how the Lord protected Jehoshaphat and the children of Israel, David, Daniel, Shadrach

Meshach, and Abednego, He will protect you. Build that relationship with Him and be faithful to Him no matter where you are, no matter how popular you are, and no matter how wealthy you are and He will be there for you. **Deuteronomy 31:6** says *"Be strong and of a good courage, fear not, nor be afraid of them: for the LORD thy God, he it is that doth go with thee; he will not fail thee, nor forsake thee"*. Be encouraged, your God has never lost a battle. He holds this world in His hand so fear not. Be bold and confident like David and decree and declare that the Lord is your rock, fortress, and deliverer.

DAY ELEVEN

According to Romans 8:37, I decree and declare that "I am more than a conqueror through Him who loves me"

Complete affirmation eleven.

All of us have been through and is going through some sort of battle in our life. Life is not perfect but our God is. We serve an omnipotent God. The God who sits high and looks low. It is important for you to know that you are not alone. God is omnipresent, He is always ready to help us with our struggles, and God is always ready to help us with our pain. Don't try to fight your battles on your own. If you fight on your own you will fail but if we fight with the power of God on our side we will always win.

To be more than conquerors is to be completely victorious at that moment. Someone needs to speak these words out loud "**The problems may seem overwhelming but I will win not with my strength but with the strength and power of almighty God**" They may come in their numbers but you *must* win. As God came through for David in his battle with the lion, the battle with the bear, and the battle with Goliath, so God will come through for you.

In 1st Samuel 17:45, David says *"Thou comest to me with a sword, and with a spear, and with a shield: but I come to thee in the name of the LORD* *of hosts, the God of the armies of Israel, whom thou hast defied."* When the fight comes use the Name. When the test comes use the Name. Use the name and demons have to flee, use the Name, and devils have to back up, use the name and pulldown and root up strongholds. You're a winner.

DAY TWELVE

According to Philippians 4:13, I decree and declare that "I can do all things through Christ who strengthens me"

Complete affirmation twelve.

There is no limit to what you can do so do not limit yourself. Neither should you allow anyone to put limits on you and put you in a box. More importantly, do not limit God. There are many who have not reached their full potential nor achieved their goals because they chose to listen to others' opinions of them. The family you were born in, the community you grew up in nor the things you have done, are as big as your God. Believers should think big. Do not think like a pigeon. Think like an eagle. A pigeon can fly to an altitude of 6000 feet but an eagle can fly to an altitude of 10,000 feet. Do not allow the pigeon-thinking people around you to hold you back. Break free and sour.

There is an eagle in all of us but you have to be deliberate to activate It., You may have to do things differently, and you may have to change your thinking and ask God to increase your faith. You're created to sour not by your strength but through Christ.

There are many examples of persons one may call *simple* and God used them to do great things. If God can use them He can use you. If they can do it, you can do it too. Step out and go start that new business, go back to school, and apply for that job. You can do it.

DAY THIRTEEN

According to Psalm 27:1 I decree and declare that "The LORD is my light and my salvation; whom shall I fear? The LORD is the strength of my life; of whom shall I be afraid?"

Complete affirmation thirteen.

Fear is not of God. The child of God should not harbor fear in his heart, no matter what is seeking to come up against you. Have no fear. In **Psalm 23:4** David says, *"Yea, though I walk through the valley of the shadow of death, I will fear no evil: for thou art with me; thy rod and thy staff they comfort me"* Like David we must have this confidence in who we are and whose we are. We are not ordinary, we are extraordinary. We are not normal, we are powerful. We are strong, we are not weak. The God we serve makes the difference. He is the Lord of lords. Not *if* but when the fights come, remember He has never lost a battle. He split the sea so the children of Israel can walk through on dry land. So build your confidence and trust in your God. He did it for me and He has already done it for you. Press through the test. God wants to take you to the next level.

DAY FOURTEEN

According to Micah 3:8, I decree and declare that "I am full of power by the spirit of the Lord"

Complete affirmation fourteen.

Once you speak about the true and living God, you're speaking about power. As children of God, we also have power; the power to walk right, the power to talk right; power to live according to the principles of God. We have the power to speak things into being. **Luke 9:1-2** says *"And He called the twelve together, and gave them power and authority over all the demons and to heal diseases. And He sent them out to proclaim the Kingdom of God and to perform healing."* This text is proof that the disciples were given supernatural power to heal the sick and cast out devils. This power was given to them by the one who has all true power and He said greater things will *we* do. This power He gave to the disciples is also extended to us.

> **Acts 5:12-16** says,
> And by the hands of the apostles were many signs and wonders wrought among the people; (and they were all with one accord in Solomon's porch. And of the rest durst no man join himself to them: but the people magnified them. And believers were the

> more added to the Lord, multitudes both of men and women.) Insomuch that they brought forth the sick into the streets, and laid them on beds and couches, that at the least the shadow of Peter passing by might overshadow some of them. There came also a multitude out of the cities round about unto Jerusalem, bringing sick folks, and them which were vexed with unclean spirits: and they were healed every one.

Those of us who are filled with the Holy Ghost have the same power to do all that was written in the text above but we need to get rid of doubt and actively use this power without delay.

We have the power to decree and declare in the name of Jesus Christ. **Acts 3:1- says**:

> Now Peter and John went up together into the temple at the hour of prayer, being the ninth hour. And a certain man lame from his mother's womb was carried, whom they laid daily at the gate of the temple which is called Beautiful, to ask alms of them that entered into the temple; who seeing Peter and John about to go into the temple asked an alms. And Peter,

fastening his eyes upon him with John, said, Look on us. And he gave heed unto them, expecting to receive something of them. Then Peter said, Silver and gold have I none; but such as I have give I thee: In the name of Jesus Christ of Nazareth rise up and walk. And he took him by the right hand, and lifted him up: and immediately his feet and ankle bones received strength. And he leaping up stood, and walked, and entered with them into the temple, walking, and leaping, and praising God. And all the people saw him walking and praising God:

Flesh and blood did not give the Apostles this power and they could not do anything of themselves. It was the Holy Ghost who gave it to them and the use of the name of Jesus Christ as there is power in the Name of Jesus. Peter said, *"such as I have given I thee in the Name of Jesus Christ"*. I also have this power; you also have this power to do this and greater. So go out and conquer your community, conquer your workplace, and conquer your country for Jesus Christ with the power given to you. "Yes, we can!"

DAY FIFTEEN

According to 2nd Timothy 1:7, I decree and declare that "God did not give me a spirit of fear, but of power, of love and of a sound mind"

Complete affirmation fifteen.

A person who has the Spirit of God has God inside them. The Spirit of God is there to help us to live a holy life and to do things according to His principles and His will. A person with the Holy Ghost has no time to entertain fear. The disciples did not display any fear so why should we? As they were fearless in proclaiming the Gospel of Jesus Christ, risking being imprisoned, beaten, and even death, we too should be just as fearless and bold. They declared that which Jesus preached and demonstrated the great commandment to love each other enough to die for them

The Spirit of God gives us power and boldness. Peter for example denied Jesus three times. Mark 14:66-72 says:

> And as Peter was beneath in the palace, there cometh one of the maids of the high priest: And when she saw Peter warming himself, she looked upon him, and said, and thou also was with Jesus of Nazareth.
>
> But he denied, saying, I know not, neither understand I what thou sayest. And he went

out into the porch; and the cock crew. And a maid saw him again, and began to say to them that stood by, this is one of them. And he denied it again. And a little after, they that stood by said again to Peter, Surely thou art one of them: for thou art a Galilaean, and thy speech agreeth thereto. But he began to curse and to swear, saying, I know not this man of whom ye speak. And the second time the cock crew. And Peter called to mind the word that Jesus said unto him, before the cock crow twice, thou shalt deny me thrice. And when he thought thereon, he wept.

Peter loved Jesus but he was afraid they would hurt him or worst take his life. But the same Peter on the day of Pentecost, when he received the Holy Ghost and power, began to speak with other tongues as the Spirit gave utterance and all who were present started to question what this meant., Some were mocking the Apostles and even thought they were drunk. But the now Holy Ghost filled, power-packed, fearless Peter in Acts 2:14-16 lifted up his voice and said unto them:

> ye men of Judea, and all that dwell at Jerusalem, be this known unto you, and

hearken to my words: For these are not drunken, as yes suppose, seeing it is but the third hour of the day, But this is that which was spoken by the prophet Joel; And it shall come to pass in the last days, saith God, I will pour out of my Spirit upon all flesh: and your sons and your daughters shall prophesy, and your young men shall see visions, and your old men shall dream dreams: And on my servants and on my handmaidens I will pour out in those days of my Spirit; and they shall prophesy: And I will shew wonders in heaven above, and signs in the earth beneath; blood, and fire, and vapour of smoke: The sun shall be turned into darkness, and the moon into blood, before the great and notable day of the Lord come: And it shall come to pass, that whosoever shall call on the name of the Lord shall be saved.

Peter started to preach the word of God with boldness on the same day he received power from on high. So where was the fear he displayed before? Fear was gone. You can, you should, and you must eliminate fear and walk in the power and authority God gave you.

DAY SIXTEEN

According to Jeremiah 29:11, I decree and declare that "God has great plans for me and I am filled with hope for a great future"

Complete affirmation sixteen.

God's plans for His children is that we prosper and be in good health even as our soul prospers. You are a child of God you're a citizen of the Kingdom of God and as a citizen in the Kingdom of God, you have access to so many uncommon favors. For instance, you have access to healing, you have access to wealth, and you have access to all you need in this life both spiritually and physically. Kingdom citizens cannot go to bed hungry because their God has a thousand cattle on hills stretched across this world.

Wherever you are you have access to it. Someone reading this book may be struggling to make ends meet but I speak to your situation right now and declare it won't always be like this. It is turning around for your good. Weeping may endure for a night but joy comes in the future. There is light at the end of the tunnel and it's not the train - it's your season of transition. Something new is coming into your life but you have to do your part.

You have to seek, prepare and wait. Your future looks bright; the King of kings wants you to have a great future. Activate your faith by standing on God's word. If He can feed five thousand from two loaves and five fishes, what can He not do for you?

Keep your faith and praise through the storm, my Brethren.

As a father, I ensure my two sons get the best education and I ensure they have a foundation for reading the word of God and praying and fasting. I get them involved in different activities to build their Godly character. I do this because I want them to have a good future. If I don't play my part it will look bad on me as a father. Our Heavenly Father and King put the word of God in play to guide us on how to get a good future one such key is found in Mathew 6:25-31 which says:

> Jesus speaking "Therefore I say to you, do not worry about your life, what you will eat or what you will drink; nor about your body, what you will put on. Is not life more than food and the body more than clothing? Look at the birds of the air, for they neither sow nor reap nor gather into barns; yet your heavenly Father feeds them. Are you not of more value than they? Which of you by worrying can add one cubit to his stature? "So why do you worry about clothing? Consider the lilies of the field, how they grow: they neither toil nor spin, and yet I say to you that even Solomon in all his glory was not arrayed like one of these. Now if God so clothes the grass of the field, which today is, and

tomorrow is thrown into the oven, *will He* not much more *clothe* you, O you of little faith? "Therefore do not worry, saying, 'What shall we eat?' or 'What shall we drink?' or 'What shall we wear?' For after all these things the Gentiles seek. For your heavenly Father knows that you need all these things. But seek first the kingdom of God and His righteousness, and all these things shall be added to you. Therefore do not worry about tomorrow, for tomorrow will worry about its own things. Sufficient for the day *is* its own trouble.

Readers, God has a great future in store for you. All you have to do is just seek first the Kingdom of God and His righteousness, then wait for His directions to you then act on His instructions and watch God work in your life and in your Ministry. Pastors whose Ministry is not growing, need to get back to basics and *seek he first*.

DAY SEVENTEEN

According to Romans 8:31 I decree and declare that "If God be for me, who can be against me"

Complete affirmation seventeen.

When the favour of God is on your life, many persons may walk away from you, including your family. Do not be disheartened. Keep your eyes on what God is doing in your life. Go after the dream He has given you. Additionally, be careful whom you share your dreams with.

People will fight you because of your dreams. You did not give yourself the gift to sing and when people hear it they feel less depressed and feel a sense of hope. Nevertheless, people will hate you because of your gift. It is God who gives man gifts. No matter how much they dislike that fact or dislike you, there is nothing they can do about it because if God be for you who can be against you?

God is your total supply, source, and guide. We are not talking about a God with eyes but cannot see. We are not talking about a God with ears that hear. We serve the all-seeing God; we serve the all-knowing God and what the enemy meant for evil God will turn it around for our Good.

Jesus never fails and once He is with you the victory is already yours – it's guaranteed.

In the Old Testament, we read about Joseph and saw how God came through for him. God continued to be with him even in prison. God will do the very same for you. We also read about Daniel, jealousy moved the heart of men to set him up for death but God came through for him while he was in the lions' den. The three Hebrew boys were also sentenced to die by fire but when the King look he asked, "Did we not cast three men bound in the fire? They answered and said yes King, the ungodly king said "**I see four men loose, walking in the midst of the fire, and they have no hurt; and the form of the fourth is like the Son of God**". **(Daniel 3:25).**

God is going to bless you in front of those who want to see you down. David put it like this, "*Thou prepares a table before me in the presence of my enemies.*" Don't pray for God to move them out of your community or out of your church or out of your place of work. Instead, ask God for the strength to endure and you will see that they cannot win because God is with you.

DAY EIGHTEEN

According to Romans 8:35-39, I decree and declare that "Nothing shall separate me from the love of Christ"

Complete affirmation eighteen.

The love Jesus Christ has for us is much deeper than that of a mother for her child. It is deeper than that of a husband for his wife or any form of friendship. The difference between the love of Christ and the love of man is that sometimes man's love is conditional. They love you for what you can do for them and once you cannot do it anymore or they do not need you, the love goes away. They may love you up to the point where you mess up but as soon as you do, they cannot be found. The love of Jesus Christ our Lord is unconditional. It is the agape love. No matter what you have done, no matter how you have messed up, once you repent and truly turn away from sin, He is waiting to welcome you back into the family of God.

Luke 15:11-32 gave details about a "prodigal son". This son was the youngest and he asked his father for his portion of his father's fortune. After receiving it, he left home (covering) and went into a strange land, and wasted his money on sinful living.

He spent it on prostitutes and maybe alcohol and 'friends'. However, when he lost it all, there were no friends around to help him. A famine came and he became desperate. He as a Jewish boy had to work in a pig pen and even ate what the pigs ate. But he came to himself and said, "I will arise and go back to my father". If you are a backslider reading this book, you're doing things you know you're not to do and it seems as if you can't stop, like this prodigal son, you need to look into yourself and shout with a loud voice **I Will Arise!**

The Bible said, when the boy was far off his father saw him and ran to him, embraced him, put a coat over him (he received back his covering), placed shoes on his feet (things were so bad the boy was barefooted) and put a ring on his finger (he received again his authority as a son). The father demonstrated that nothing can prevent him from loving his son. Similarly, nothing can separate us from God's love. He loves us to the utmost and He is faithful and just to forgive us and cleanse us from all unrighteousness. If God has forgiven me who are you to condemn me?

In the story, the eldest brother was critical and not happy about the sinner's return. You may have backslidden and returned to God and you are now promoted over someone who did not leave the church and persons may be talking about you and not showing you love or welcoming you with open arms be encouraged and *pray until something happen* (PUSH) and always remember, it was Christ who died and not that critical person or persons who are unwilling to forgive you. The Bible states that all have sinned and come short of the Glory of God but through our repentance and His love and forgiveness, we shall live in His presence.

DAY NINETEEN

According to Philippians 1:6, I decree and declare that "He who hath began a good work in me shall complete it"

Complete affirmation nineteen.

Whatever God promises you, whatever He said he will do for you, He will do it. It may take much longer than we hope or think, but He will complete it. On this journey called life, you may encounter difficulties such as sickness, heartache, and pain but don't lean to your own understanding put your trust always in Jesus Christ. I call him the ***fix-it Jesus.*** Whatever you're going through, Jesus can fix it. The fixing process may have started a week ago or even a month ago and you're anxious for the final result, but be patient and wait. He will complete what He has started. There was a lady who was paralyzed from a car accident. She had to move around in a wheelchair but she kept on worshipping God. She went to a revival and when the Minister identified her, he asked her husband (who was a pastor) to take her to the altar.

The worship was rich, and the power of God came upon her. Before that day she could not feel any sensation in her foot but when the Minister touched her foot she could feel his hand.

God started a work in her. She was helped out of the wheelchair and started to move her feet and walk with help. She was not completely healed there and then. It took up to three weeks for the healing process to complete. God had started a good work in her and He completed it. God could have done it immediately but He has His timing and we need to respect that and be encouraged that whatever He starts He will finish no matter how long it may take. When doubts come and they sometimes will just hold on to faith and His word. If your faith is low, ask Jesus Christ to increase your faith. He will.

DAY TWENTY

According to Philippians 4:6, I decree and declare that "I am anxious for nothing, but in everything, by prayer and supplication, with thanksgiving, I will make my request known to God"

Complete affirmation twenty.

When you know God for yourself, when you have built a relationship with Him, no matter what comes your way, you will have no doubt that God will bring you through. All we need to do is pray to Him and give Him thanks in advance for whatever we have prayed about. The Bible tells us 'without faith it is impossible to please God'. All the great men and women of God were able to operate in the realm of the Spirit because they knew their God. Do you really have a relationship with God? Do you really know who God is? Job did. The Bible describes Job as a perfect and upright man. Job feared God and shunned evil. Job was wealthy and was great in his country but he honored God.

The Bible tells us that Job lost all his children. He lost his animals and back to back he received bad news after bad news. Job did not curse God. Job 1: 20-21 says *"Then Job arose, and rent his mantle, and shaved his head, and fell down upon the ground, and worshipped, And said, Naked came I out of my mother's womb, and naked shall I return thither: the LORD gave, and the LORD hath taken away; blessed be the name of the LORD"*

Job brought his situation to God, but things did not change immediately. In fact, it appears they got worst. What do you do when you have been praying to God to restore your marriage, to heal your body, to save your child but instead of things getting better they get worst? What do you do? As Christians, we should continue to pray, and continue to trust God.

Things got so bad for Job that his wife told him to curse God and die. At this point, the enemy had touched his flesh but Job said, *"Thou speakest as one of the foolish woman speaketh. What? Shall we receive good at the hand of God, and shall we not receive evil? In all this did not Job sin with his lips"* **Job 2:10.** Job friends came to visit him and could not say a word for over a week. They did not know what to say because of the state he was in. They started to wonder what sins he committed. We need to know that sometimes bad things may happen to good people. But God will make a way and if He brings you to it, He will bring you through it.

Job remained faithful. Job said 'I will wait till my change come" and God gave him double for his trouble. All the animals he lost, God gave him double. God gave him ten more children. This is a word for someone reading this book at this time. Do not be anxious about the state of your life, or what you're dealing with. Instead, fast, pray, worship, give thanks, and wait. God will do it and give you victory because the victory belongs to Jesus.

DAY TWENTY ONE

According to Psalm 103:3, I decree and declare that "My God heals all diseases"

Complete affirmation twenty one.

When God created Adam and placed him in the Garden of Eden, there was no sickness. Sickness entered when man sinned. Sicknesses such as high blood pressure, stroke, cancer, and heart disease are all that I will call consequences of sin. There are two types of healing: instant healing and progressive healing. An example of instant healing I observed personally was when a man was taken to our church on a stretcher. He could not walk, he was brought to the back of the church and when we prayed he said he felt something moving in his body. It was the power of God. He was healed instantly by God. The man who came into the church not walking; was able to walk to the pool and be baptized in the Name of Jesus Christ.

The Bible has several examples of instantaneous healing but I will bring two to your attention. The first is the woman who had the issue of blood for twelve years.

Luke 8:43-48 says:

And a woman having an issue of blood twelve years, which had spent all her living upon physicians, neither could be healed of any, Came behind him, and touched the border of his garment: and immediately her issue of blood stanched. And Jesus said, who touched me? When all denied, Peter and they that were with him said, Master, the multitude throng thee and press thee, and sayest thou, who touched me? And Jesus said, somebody hath touched me: for I perceive that virtue is gone out of me. And when the woman saw that she was not hid, she came trembling, and falling down before him, she declared unto him before all the people for what cause she had touched him, and how she was healed immediately. And he said unto her, Daughter, be of good comfort: thy faith hath made thee whole; go in peace".

What she did was illegal. She was considered unclean but she was desperate for a change and her only hope was in Jesus Christ. Jesus came through for her. Someone reading this book may have been suffering for a long time with a similar situation and the doctors fail and you may feel there is no hope but may I submit to you: ***there is Hope for you in Jesus***. He can heal you at this moment just as He healed that woman.

The next example was the woman who was bent over for eighteen years. The Bible says that Jesus was teaching in the synagogue on the Sabbath and while he was teaching he saw a woman who had an infirmity for eighteen years, she could not walk upright but she was still going to hear the word of

God. Jesus called her and said "Woman thou art loosed from thine infirmities" and the Bible says immediately she was made straight (**Luke 13:10-13**).

There is also progressive healing. An example of this type of healing can be seen on day 20 with this lady who was confined to a wheelchair for twenty-two years and God healed her. **Mark 8:22-25** gave another example of progressive healing. The text says *"And he cometh to Bethsaida; and they bring a blind man unto him, and besought him to touch him. And he took the blind man by the hand, and led him out of the town; and when he had spit on his eyes, and put his hands upon him, he asked him if he saw ought. And he looked up, and said, I see men as trees, walking. After that he put his hands again upon his eyes, and made him look up: and he was restored, and saw every man clearly"*

Jesus had the power to heal him in one go. But this is an example to someone who is sick to not lose hope. It may not come when you want it to be done. But if you believe and wait with a praise He will do it for you.

- Jesus healed the leper Matthew 8:2-3

    "And, behold, there came a leper and worshipped him, saying, Lord, if thou wilt, thou canst make me clean. And Jesus put

forth his hand, and touched him, saying, I will: be thou clean. And immediately his leprosy was cleansed"

- Jesus healed the centurion servant Matthew 8:5-13

    "And when Jesus was entered into Capernaum, there came unto him a centurion, beseeching him. And saying, Lord, my servant lieth at home sick of the palsy, grievously tormented. And Jesus saith unto him, I will come and heal him. The centurion answered and said, Lord, I am not worthy that thou shouldest come under my roof: but speak the word only, and my servant shall be healed. For I am a man under authority, having soldiers under me: and I say to this man, Go, and he goeth; and to another, Come, and he cometh; and to my servant, Do this, and he doeth it. When Jesus heard it, he marveled , and said to them that followed, Verily I say unto you, I have not found so great faith, no, not in Israel. And I say unto you, That many shall come from the east and west, and shall sit down with Abraham, and Isaac, and Jacob, in the kingdom of heaven. But the children of the kingdom shall be cast out into outer darkness: there shall be weeping and gnashing of teeth. And Jesus said unto the centurion, Go thy way; and as thou hast believed, so be it done unto thee. And his servant was healed in the selfsame hour"

- Jesus healed Peter's mother in law Matthew 8:14-15

  "And when Jesus was come into Peter's house, he saw his wife's mother laid, and sick of a fever. And he touched her hand, and the fever left her: and she arose, and ministered unto them"

- Jesus healed many persons who were sick and also delivered the possessed with His words, Matthew 8:16

  "When the even was come, they brought unto him many that were possessed with devils: and he cast out the spirits with his word, and healed all that were sick"

Isaiah said by his stripes we are healed but 1st Peter says by his stripes ye were healed. When compassion and love go out, virtue comes in. Agree with someone and let faith arise for your healing.

Matthew 18:19 says *"Again I say unto you, That if two of you shall agree on earth as touching anything that they shall ask, it shall be done for them of my Father which is in heaven."* God wants to heal you but you have to be desperate and deliberate. Agree with someone by faith for your healing and God will do it.

I see healing as both a gift and a right for citizens of the Kingdom of God. You have full access so claim it and receive it in Jesus Name.

TESTIMONY OF PROPHETIC DECLARATION

There are several persons that I know who have used this formula of decreeing and declaring things over their lives and God made it a reality. I have also experienced the power of prophetic declaration myself. I will share a few powerful testimonies including two of my own to demonstrate that this works. The prophetic declaration is not a thing of the past only. It is also revenant today.

Testimony of Elder Stevie Barnett 1

When I was in high school, I always wanted to work in a bank. The ladies in the bank looked so poised and beautiful and the gentlemen looked very sharp. Moreover, I wanted to work in the bank because I thought that it would normally close early compared to other places of employment. I realized that after completing my Bachelor of Science Degree, I still had the desire to work in the Bank.

I remember one evening Missionary Chevanese Kelly and I were coming from church and I went to

The National Commercial Bank door and I held the handle of the door. I asked Missionary Kelly to agree with me and at that moment I decree and declared that I will work at The National Commercial Bank. A member of our church who was a vendor at the bank door chased us away, but the declaration was already done.

A few months later I saw an advertisement for employment in the local newspaper from The National Commercial Bank. I applied and I received a job at The National Commercial Bank. I worked at The National Commercial Bank for over 10 years. Declaration works!

If God did it for me he can do it for you.

- ➤ Decree and declare for that dream job
- ➤ Decree and declare for that dream house
- ➤ decree and declare for a child
- ➤ decree and declare for your debts to be canceled and your financing to be improved
- ➤ Decree and declare that your children will get saved
- ➤ Decree and declare that your spouse will give his or her life to God

        It shall be done in Jesus Name.

Testimony of Elder Stevie Barnett Two

On March 14^{th,} 2023 I was stopped and given a traffic ticket by a Police officer. I was given a ticket because I did not come to a complete stop at a stop sign. I asked the officer to give me a chance but he would not have it, the value of the ticket was JA$10,000. I took the ticket and proceeded. I perused the ticket and realized the last date to pay at the tax office was April 13^{th,} 2023. I decided that I would make the payment on the morning of April 12^{th,} 2023.

I was also slated to leave the Island for an International Congress in the United States of America. My flight was from Montego Bay and I live in Kingston and the time for the flight was 3:45 pm. The drive from Kingston to Montego Bay was approximately three hours. The line at the tax office was long and time was running out on me so I decided not to pay the ticket on that date. I opted to pay for the ticket at the traffic court on April 24^{th,} 2023.

The court start time was 10 am and I ensure I was early. The police officer on duty called five names including my name and we all lined up and entered the courtroom. At least one person who was in the courtroom before me had a similar offense as mine and the judge told him to pay JA$20,000 or 5 days in jail. A few others were also fined for their offense. The clerk then called one of the people who entered the court with me, his case was dismissed because of an error by the officer who issued the ticket.

I should have mentioned I did not have the JA$10,000 to pay the fine, I only had JA$30,000 my wife gave me to work on her car. When it was almost my time to face the Judge, I remembered the power of declaration. I declared in my mind that I will not pay more than the JA$10,000 because that is the trend, the Judge usually charges a higher amount than the ticket value. I quickly declared again that I will not pay anything for this ticket.

It was my time to face the Judge, my name was called and I entered the dock, the Judge told me good afternoon and I responded. At this stage, the clerk of the court started to read the offense but to my surprise, the clerk paused and recommended that the case be dismissed (she gave a reason) but, I believe with all my heart it was the power of declaration in the Name of Jesus at work. The Judge said "Mr. Barnett you're free to go" I replied, thank you Judge, and thank you, Jesus. I did not have to borrow money from my wife to pay that bill. To God be the glory, great things he has done.

Testimony of Sister Venada Dillon

In 2002 I had discomfort in my throat and mouth. There was an unusual dryness in my mouth and there was a hollow sound when I swallow. I went to the General Practitioners and they couldn't diagnose the cause, I went to the ENT specialists at the University Hospital of the West Indies for four years. Several blood tests were done, and Biopsy was done on my lips but the doctors could not diagnose the illness. My saliva was almost at the point of being dried. I began to speak to my body, I began to speak to my salivary gland and I decreed and declared that I am healed.

I was tired of this sickness, I spent a lot to correct this sickness, but the doctors could not diagnose the issue. The God of Abraham, the God of Isaac, and the God of Jacob healed my throat and mouth, although everything came back to normal through constant prophetic declaration. The healing did not take place immediately and that's okay. God does not work according to our program, God works according to His timing. Hallelujah!

Testimony of Minister Owen Boswell

Five years ago when I migrated to America, there is a particular building I set my eyes on because I was advised of the attractive remuneration and fringe benefits. For several years I decreed and declared that I must work in that building. I am now doing my third year in this building. To God be the glory, great things he has done. Because of security protocol, I am unable to disclose the building but, I can truly testify that declaration works.

Testimony of Pastor and Lady Simone McKenzie

I got married to the love of my life in 2008. As with any other couple, we desired a child and prayed consistently hoping it would happen. For years we have laid hands on many women and watched them conceive through the power of God. But for us, it was like Sarah and Abraham.

When things looked hopeless and impossible God showed up. After fourteen years of marriage, we were blessed with the most beautiful baby girl. I know you might be wondering, how after so long but, sometimes the miracles are in the waiting. If you have been waiting on God, don't lose hope. The greater the wait, the greater the miracle.

CONCLUSION

There are many people who are not living their best life now because of what they hear. Some may hear and meditate on; you're not good enough, you're not going to turn out to be anything good, you're not smart enough, you're not tall enough, and you're not beautiful enough. Some may even also have negative self-thoughts and entertain them. As a result of all those words and negative thoughts, many people live below the standard God wants them to live. Many persons even die before accomplishing the greatness that they were born with.

Because of all that was written in the above paragraph, this is why a book like this is important. Please understand that it takes words to combat words. Each time you open this book and speak out loud the declarations, you are combating all those negative words you heard before. **Romans 10:17** says *"So then faith cometh by hearing, and hearing by the word of God"*. Therefore, the more you read the word of God, the more you will believe that He can heal you, the more you will believe that you're the head and not the tail, above and not beneath, lend and not borrow, blessed and highly favored. What you hear can either allow you to be faithful or fearful.

Jesus gave us a perfect example of using words in Matthew 4:2-10;

> And when He had fasted forty days and forty nights, afterward He was hungry. Now when the tempter came to Him, he said, "If you are the Son of God, command that these stones become bread." But He answered and said, "It is written, 'Man shall not live by bread alone, but by every word that proceeds from the mouth of God.' " Then the devil took Him up into the holy city, set Him on the pinnacle of the temple, and said to Him, "If You are the Son of God, throw Yourself down. For it is written: 'He shall give His angels charge over you, 'and, 'In *their* hands they shall bear you up, Lest you dash your foot against a stone.' " Jesus said to him, "It is written again, 'You shall not tempt the LORD your God.' "Again, the devil took Him up on an exceedingly high mountain, and showed Him all the kingdoms of the world and their glory. And he said to Him, "All these things I will give you if you will fall down and worship me." Then Jesus said

to him, "Away with you, Satan! For it is written, 'You shall worship the LORD your God, and Him only you shall serve.

In all these instances, Jesus uses words to combat words - "words on words". It takes words to combat words. Songwriter Donald Lawrence (2006) puts it this way:

> Sometimes you have to encourage yourself
> Sometimes you have to speak victory during the test
> And no matter how you feel
> Speak the word, and you will be healed
> Speak over yourself
> Encourage yourself in the Lord
> (© Q. W. Publishing, Bridge Building Music Inc.)

The question may be asked, why I stopped at twenty one days. The first reason is that this was the number laid on my heart by the Lord. The second reason is that one method to build habits is to do something for twenty one days straight. It is believed that if you can do something for three weeks straight you will develop a new habit. Once you do an activity for twenty-one days and continue another ninety days it will become a permanent life habit. I am challenging all readers to change their perspective and begin to think about life in a positive way by reading these twenty one Prophetic Declarations over your life consistently for twenty one days and then ninety days, declare these words, and watch what God will do in your life. Your life will never be the same. It's your time to walk in your overflow, it's your time to walk in your winning season. But you have to do something, you have to speak the words. God said it, we believe it and it is done.

APPENDIX

Affirmation Journal
Declaration Journal
Declaration word search

Affirmation Journal

AFFIRMATION ONE

Date: _____ I _____

Decree and Declare

God Said It I believe it, it is done

"No weapon that is formed against me shall prosper"

AFFIRMATION TWO

Date: _____ I _____

Decree and Declare

God Said It I believe it, it is done

"I am blessed in the city and I am blessed in the field"

AFFIRMATION THREE

Date: _____ I _____

Decree and Declare

God Said It I believe it, it is done

> "My basket and my store shall be blessed"

AFFIRMATION FOUR

Date: _____ I _____

Decree and Declare

God Said It I believe it, it is done

> "My basket and my store shall be blessed"

AFFIRMATION FIVE

Date: _____ I _____

Decree and Declare

God Said It I believe it, it is done

"I shall be blessed when I goest out and when I comest in"

AFFIRMATION SIX

Date: _____ I _____

Decree and Declare

God Said It I believe it, it is done

"My enemies which come out against me one way will flee before me seven ways"

AFFIRMATION SEVEN

Date: _____ I _____

Decree and Declare

God Said It
I believe it, it is done

"All that I set my hand unto shall be blessed"

AFFIRMATION SEVEN

Date: _____ I _____

Decree and Declare

God Said It
I believe it, it is done

"All that I set my hand unto shall be blessed"

AFFIRMATION EIGHT

Date: _____ I _____

Decree and Declare

God Said It I believe it, it is done

"God will bless all the works of my hand, I will lend and not borrow"

AFFIRMATION NINE

Date: _____ I _____

Decree and Declare

God Said It I believe it, it is done

"I will be the head and not the tail, I will be above and not beneath"

AFFIRMATION TEN

Date: _____ I _____
Decree and Declare

> God Said It I believe it, it is done

"The Lord is my rock and my fortress and my deliverer"

AFFIRMATION ELEVEN

Date: _____ I _____
Decree and Declare

> God Said It I believe it, it is done

"I am more than a conqueror through Him who loves me"

AFFIRMATION TWELVE

Date: _____ I _____
Decree and Declare

> God Said It I believe it, it is done

"I can do all things through Christ who strengthens me"

AFFIRMATION THIRTEEN

Date: _____ I _____
Decree and Declare

> God Said It I believe it, it is done

"The LORD is my light and my salvation; whom shall I fear? The LORD is the

AFFIRMATION FOURTEEN

Date: _____ I _____

Decree and Declare

God Said It I believe it, it is done

"I am full of power by the spirit of the Lord"

AFFIRMATION FIFTEEN

Date: _____ I _____

Decree and Declare

God Said It I believe it, it is done

"God did not give me a spirit of fear, but of power, of love and of a sound mind"

AFFIRMATION SIXTEEN

Date: _____ I _____
Decree and Declare

> God Said It — I believe it, it is done

"God has great plans for me and I am filled with hope for a great future"

AFFIRMATION SEVENTEEN

Date: _____ I _____
Decree and Declare

> God Said It — I believe it, it is done

"If God be for me, who can be against me"

AFFIRMATION EIGHTEEN

Date: _____ I _____

Decree and Declare

God Said It I believe it, it is done

"Nothing shall separate me from the love of Christ"

AFFIRMATION NINETEEN

Date: _____ I _____

Decree and Declare

God Said It I believe it, it is done

"He who hath began a good work in me shall complete it"

AFFIRMATION TWENTY

Date: _____ I _____
Decree and Declare

God Said It I believe it, it is done

"I am anxious for nothing, but in everything, by prayer and supplication, with thanksgiving, I will make my request known to God"

AFFIRMATION TWENTY ONE

Date: _____ I _____
Decree and Declare

God Said It I believe it, it is done

"My God heals all diseases"

Declaration Journal

DECLARATION

Date declaration made: _____

> God Said It I believe it, it is done

I _____

Decree and declare;

_____

_____

_____

_____

_____

_____

_____

_____

_____

Date declaration manifested: _____

DECLARATION

Date declaration made: _____

God Said It — I believe it, it is done

I _____

Decree and declare;

_____

_____

_____

_____

_____

_____

_____

_____

_____

Date declaration manifested: _____

DECLARATION

Date declaration made: _____

God Said It I believe it, it is done

I _____
Decree and declare;
_____
_____
_____
_____
_____
_____
_____
_____

Date declaration manifested: _____

DECLARATION

Date declaration made: _____

God Said It I believe it, it is done

I _____

Decree and declare;

_____
_____
_____
_____
_____
_____
_____
_____
_____

Date declaration manifested: _____

DECLARATION

Date declaration made: _____

God Said It I believe it, it is done

I _____

Decree and declare;

_____
_____
_____
_____
_____
_____
_____
_____

Date declaration manifested: _____

DECLARATION

Date declaration made: _____

**God Said It
I believe it, it is done**

I _____

Decree and declare;

_____

_____

_____

_____

_____

_____

_____

Date declaration manifested: _____

DECLARATION

Date declaration made: _____

God Said It I believe it, it is done

I _____

Decree and declare;

_____
_____
_____
_____
_____
_____
_____
_____
_____

Date declaration manifested: _____

DECLARATION

Date declaration made: _____

God Said It I believe it, it is done

I _____

Decree and declare;

_____

_____

_____

_____

_____

_____

_____

_____

Date declaration manifested: _____

DECLARATION

Date declaration made: _____

God Said It I believe it, it is done

I _____

Decree and declare;

_____
_____
_____
_____
_____
_____
_____
_____
_____

Date declaration manifested: _____

DECLARATION

Date declaration made: _____

God Said It I believe it, it is done

I _____

Decree and declare;

_____
_____
_____
_____
_____
_____
_____
_____

Date declaration manifested: _____

DECLARATION

Date declaration made: _____

God Said It I believe it, it is done

I _____

Decree and declare;

_____

_____

_____

_____

_____

_____

_____

_____

Date declaration manifested: _____

DECLARATION

Date declaration made: _____

God Said It I believe it, it is done

I _____

Decree and declare;

_____
_____
_____
_____
_____
_____
_____
_____

Date declaration manifested: _____

Declaration word search

DECLARATION WORD SEARCH

L	P	F	W	M	W	E	O	T	R	A	E	G	F	V
B	Q	H	Y	G	C	B	V	K	J	T	N	P	E	V
D	E	C	R	E	E	J	L	P	G	A	U	V	W	U
F	H	B	S	F	V	S	O	E	S	M	N	W	S	N
R	W	E	A	O	P	U	D	J	S	H	D	H	N	Z
U	E	O	B	R	A	V	Z	E	Q	S	A	C	W	K
I	A	P	X	M	G	B	Y	S	F	S	E	L	R	N
T	P	C	P	E	A	G	P	O	P	I	D	D	L	F
P	O	I	I	D	I	Z	D	A	C	G	E	T	B	E
W	N	F	A	H	N	S	F	E	C	Z	K	L	O	T
W	B	O	P	X	S	V	Z	C	C	G	X	A	D	K
T	V	K	N	X	T	Q	C	R	C	L	C	P	Y	D
N	M	F	P	R	O	S	P	E	R	Q	A	D	U	Y
J	Q	P	O	N	S	F	C	I	T	Y	Z	R	A	G
O	X	T	F	X	V	Q	C	T	E	T	P	S	E	O

Declare   again   prosper

Blessed   decree   formed

Shall   weapon   fruit

Body

NOTES

NOTES

Made in the USA
Middletown, DE
17 April 2024